To:_____

From:_____

Date:_____

PRECIOUS MOMENTS

Twelve Days of Christmas

Baker Books

A Division of Baker Book House Co
Grand Rapids, Michigan 49516

Art © 1979, 1981, 1987, 1996 by Precious Moments, Inc.
Text © 1998 by Baker Book House

Published by Baker Books
a division of Baker Book House Company
P.O. Box 6287, Grand Rapids, MI 49516-6287

Printed in the United States of America

ISBN 0-8010-4410-3

Library of Congress Cataloging-in-Publication Data is on
file at the Library of Congress, Washington, DC.

For current information about all releases from Baker Book
House, visit our web site:
                    http://www.bakerbooks.com

*C*hristmas is coming! It's time to decorate the tree and practice singing holiday songs. Christmas is such a fun time of sharing love and holiday cheer with family and friends. Just as God gave us a very special gift at Christmas, we give gifts to each other too.

People have celebrated Christmas with songs and gifts for many years. In fact, at one time they used to celebrate Christmas for twelve whole days!

A special song tells the story of twelve gifts for the twelve days of Christmas. And we still sing that cheerful song today. As you read the words to the song, look for the special gift on each page. And remember to share your Christmas cheer with the people you love too.

On the first day of Christmas
my true love gave to me . . .

a partridge in a pear tree.

On the second day of Christmas
my true love gave to me . . .

two turtledoves
and a partridge in a pear tree.

On the third day of Christmas
my true love gave to me . . .

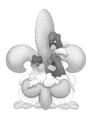

three French hens,
two turtledoves,
and a partridge in a pear tree.

On the fourth day of Christmas
my true love gave to me . . .

four calling birds,
three French hens,
two turtledoves,
and a partridge in a pear tree.

On the fifth day of Christmas
my true love gave to me . . .

five golden rings,
four calling birds,
three French hens,
two turtledoves,
and a partridge in a pear tree.

*O*n the sixth day of Christmas
my true love gave to me . . .

six geese a-laying,
five golden rings,
four calling birds,
three French hens,
two turtledoves,
and a partridge in a pear tree.

On the seventh day of Christmas
my true love gave to me . . .

seven swans a-swimming,
six geese a-laying,
five golden rings,
four calling birds,
three French hens,
two turtledoves,
and a partridge in a pear tree.

On the eighth day of Christmas
my true love gave to me . . .

eight maids a-milking,
seven swans a-swimming,
six geese a-laying,
five golden rings,
four calling birds,
three French hens,
two turtledoves,
and a partridge in a pear tree.

On the ninth day of Christmas
my true love gave to me . . .

nine ladies dancing,
eight maids a-milking,
seven swans a-swimming,
six geese a-laying,
five golden rings,
four calling birds,
three French hens,
two turtledoves,
and a partridge in a pear tree.

On the tenth day of Christmas
my true love gave to me . . .

ten lords a-leaping,
nine ladies dancing,
eight maids a-milking,
seven swans a-swimming,
six geese a-laying,
five golden rings,
four calling birds,
three French hens,
two turtledoves,
and a partridge in a pear tree.

On the eleventh day of Christmas
my true love gave to me . . .

eleven pipers piping,
ten lords a-leaping,
nine ladies dancing,
eight maids a-milking,
seven swans a-swimming,
six geese a-laying,
five golden rings,
four calling birds,
three French hens,
two turtledoves,
and a partridge in a pear tree.

On the twelfth day of Christmas
my true love gave to me . . .

twelve drummers drumming,
eleven pipers piping,
ten lords a-leaping,
nine ladies dancing,
eight maids a-milking,
seven swans a-swimming,
six geese a-laying,
five golden rings,
four calling birds,
three French hens,
two turtledoves,
and a partridge in a pear tree.

$\mathcal{N}$ow that you have read about the twelve days of Christmas, think about the special gifts of loving, caring, and sharing that you can give others this Christmas. But don't stop there! Keep giving those gifts for even more than twelve days. Give them all year long!